Using stories
to teach
Punctuation

Ages 6–7

Jonny Zucker was a primary school teacher for eight years, in addition to being a football coach. He now writes full time and has published over 50 children's and educational books.

Wendy Dixon taught for 27 years in London primary schools, including 15 years as a head teacher. She is now an educational consultant and writer.

Published by
Hopscotch Educational Publishing Ltd
Unit 2, The Old Brushworks, 56 Pickwick Road, Corsham,
Wiltshire SN13 9BX
Tel: 01249 701701

© 2006 Hopscotch Educational Publishing

Written by Jonny Zucker and Wendy Dixon
Series design by Blade Communications
Cover illustration by Debbie Clark
Illustrated by Steph Dix
Printed by Cle-print

ISBN 1 905390 23 8

Jonny Zucker and Wendy Dixon hereby assert their moral right to be identified as the authors of this work in accordance with the Copyright, Designs and Patents Act, 1988.

Acknowlededgments

Every effort has been made to trace the owners of copyright of material in this book and the publisher apologises for any inadvertent omissions. Any persons claiming copyright for any material should contact the publisher who will be happy to pay the permission fees agreed between them and who will amend the information in this book on any subsequent reprint.

PUNCTUATION CHALLENGE

Contents

Introduction

Using stories

As teachers we often struggle to be inspiring when teaching the basic rules of punctuation and sentence construction. How could teaching this area be made more interesting for both children and teachers? After much discussion we came up with the idea of using exciting stories to grab and hold children's attention.

These, however, were not just going to be one-off stories. They would all be linked by two central characters, named Emily and Jack. There is a scene-setter which is relevant to both the Ages 5–6 book and the Ages 6–7 book. In this story Emily and Jack discover an old chest in Emily's loft. The label on it says DO NOT OPEN – KEEP OUT. Of course, being inquisitive children, they open the chest and thus the adventures begin. Each new story begins with them taking an object out of the chest, at which point a mist swirls round and they are taken on a different adventure. You will need to read the scene-setter to the children the first time you use these books in class and return to it frequently.

We wanted the adventures to work on two levels: firstly as a gripping story for the readers; secondly for each story to contain one main learning objective as its central focus, with lots of strong visual cues.

For example, for Emily and Jack (and the children listening to the story) to find out about question marks, we created a story called *The dark tunnel*. In this story Emily and Jack discover that the only way to escape from the tunnel is to use question marks after questions. Each time they do, they activate one of a series of question mark-shaped lights, which show them the way out.

About the books in this series

We have highlighted the 12 Literacy Strategy Learning Objectives that are central to Key Stage 1 children's understanding and progress in this area of literacy. The Ages 5–6 book contains six objectives from the Year 1 objectives. The Ages 6–7 book contains six objectives from the Year 2 objectives. They are as follows:

Year 1 (ages 5–6) learning objectives
- Know that a sentence needs a beginning and an end.
- Use a question mark at the end of a question.
- Use a capital letter when writing I.
- Use capitals for emphasis.
- Put a full stop at the end of a sentence.

- Use a capital at the start of a sentence, names, place names, days of the week and months.

Year 2 (ages 6–7) learning objectives
- Know that exclamation marks make words strong and powerful.
- Use speech marks to catch spoken words.
- Know that there are many different ways to ask questions.
- Use commas in lists and with speech marks.
- Know that organisational devices get things organised.
- Know that speech and thought can be written in bubbles.

For each learning objective there is a 12-page unit of work. Each unit comprises:
- a four-page Emily and Jack story (maximum 600 words in the Ages 5–6 book, maximum 800 words in the Ages 6–7 book);
- two pages of teachers' notes;
- six pages of activities relating to the stories.

Within the six activity pages are two core activities that have been differentiated for three ability levels. 1A and 2A are for emergent readers and those who need support. 1B and 2B are for more confident readers. 1C and 2C are for able and more able readers.

A teacher who works through all twelve units will have covered the most essential components of Key Stage 1 sentence formation and punctuation.

On the facing page are synopses of all the stories and on page 6 the scene-setter which introduces the children to Emily and Jack's adventures.

The 'Memory joggers' on the last page of the book list the learning objectives of each story.

The teachers' notes

These are set out using the following headings:

Intended learning
Explains the learning objective for the story.

Preparation and resources
Lists necessary resources and suggests useful preparation for the lesson.

Starting point

Sets the story's scene for the whole class.

Read the story

Suggestions to help you read the story with maximum emphasis to underpin the key learning objective.

Lower order questions

Examples of simple questions that require short answers.

Higher order questions

Examples of open-ended questions to challenge able and more able children.

Points to note

Specific points relating to key aspects of the learning objective.

Group oral work

Interactive questions to reinforce the learning objective.

The activity sheets

Tips for introducing the six differentiated activity sheets.

Plenary

Suggestions for whole class opportunities to reinforce the learning objective and its link to the story.

Cross-curricular activities

Suggested activities where the main idea of the story and its learning objective can be revisited within a different framework. These are particularly beneficial for those children who may be reluctant learners during specified literacy lessons but willing participants in other subject areas.

Story synopses

Exclamation marks – *Polta and the space war*
Year 2 Term 1

Emily and Jack are involved in a space war. Enemy Pintons are attacking their craft. The giant woman Polta shows them how exclamation marks will defeat the enemy. After winning the battle they are in for a shock when they can't see their own planet – Earth.

Speech marks – *Diving in the deep*
Year 2 Term 2

Dressed in diving suits, Emily and Jack collect fishing hooks from the ocean bed. They need the hooks to catch phrases from Noisy Beach to return the power of speech to the crowds on Silent Beach. Can Emily and Jack succeed or will the people be under the pirates' curse of silence for ever?

Question words – *Escape from the tower*
Year 2 Term 3

Emily and Jack are trapped in the Tower of Questions. A huge beast bars their escape. Emily and Jack find 'question words' to feed to it. If the beast eats enough and falls asleep, will Emily and Jack have enough courage to escape past the sleeping beast?

Commas – *The Queen's banquet*
Year 2 Term 1

Emily and Jack are in the dining room of a castle. Emily has to write the menu but the chalk won't write commas. Jack has to trim the royal wigs but things go wrong. Will Emily and Jack find a solution?

Organisation devices – *The wild zoo*
Year 2 Term 2

Emily and Jack are in a chaotic zoo. All the visitors have ended up in the wrong places. Emily and Jack restore order by using a bulleted list to organise the rescue of all the people.

Speech and thought bubbles – *Bubble up*
Year 2 Term 3

Emily and Jack are in a canyon; the sides are too steep to climb. They are hungry, thirsty and frightened. With only a packet of bubblegum each, is there any hope of escape?

The chest in the loft

"Pay attention, you two!"

Best friends Emily and Jack stopped whispering. They looked at their teacher, Mr Townsend.

"I'm trying to teach the class punctuation," boomed Mr Townsend, "but as usual you two aren't listening!"

Punctuation lessons weren't their favourite thing in school. Emily liked PE; Jack liked art.

Mr Townsend looked at his watch and sighed. "Well, it's home time now anyway. Coats on everyone and walk to the gate."

As Emily and Jack walked past Mr Townsend's desk he looked at them crossly, saying, "I've told you two before; you must listen in class or you'll never learn anything."

Emily and Jack nodded, walked quietly out of the classroom, then dashed to Emily's mum's car.

"Hi, how was your day?" she asked as they clambered in.

"OK," they said together.

"Just OK?" asked Mrs Ashcroft.

"It was fine, Mum," replied Emily, not mentioning that Mr Townsend had told them off for not listening. Again.

When they reached Emily's house, Emily whispered an idea to Jack. "Let's go up to the loft. It's spooky up there. We might find something interesting."

"Cool," grinned Jack.

Emily took the walking stick from the cupboard to reach up for the loft hatch. She yanked the handle. The hatch opened and the ladder came creaking down.

Emily climbed the ladder first. Jack followed carefully.

"What are you two doing?" shouted Mrs Ashcroft from the kitchen.

"We're just going into the loft, Mum," Emily called back. "Jack's never seen a loft."

The chest in the loft

"OK," called her mum, "but be careful!"

The loft smelt dusty and musty.

"What's up here?" asked Jack as his eyes adjusted to the gloom.

"Don't know," whispered Emily. "I've never really looked."

Jack gazed round. There were old suitcases, cardboard boxes, books, magazines, broken tennis rackets and cricket bats. Jack could just make out some oars, a tangle of fishing nets and even a guitar.

"Hey, over here!" Emily suddenly called. Jack picked his way over to where Emily was sitting. On the floor in front of her was a wooden chest. On the lid of the chest, in dirty white capital letters, were the words: DO NOT OPEN – KEEP OUT.

"Let's open it," said Emily.

"No way!" replied Jack. "Read what it says! It could be something dangerous!"

"Don't be stupid. It can't hurt to look," said Emily. "Anyway, that writing's so old it won't mean anything now."

"We shouldn't," muttered Jack.

But it was too late. Emily was already lifting the lid. It creaked back stiffly on the rusty hinges. Inside there was a great collection of stuff but one thing immediately caught Jack's eye.

"Look at that!" he whispered excitedly. "Down there in the corner."

As soon as he lifted the object out the chest lid slammed shut.

Emily and Jack looked at each other in shock.

Suddenly they were surrounded by a swirling blue mist and they felt themselves being pulled upwards at an incredible speed...

Exclamation marks

Intended learning
- To understand how an exclamation mark affects the power of the preceding words.
- To know how to form exclamation marks.

Preparation and resources
- On the board write the words and symbols:

  Full stop .

  Exclamation mark !
- Write the following words and phrases, as large as possible, on half sheets of A4:

Sit down.	Sit down!
Come in.	Come in!
Yes.	Yes!
No.	No!
Line up.	Line up!
I will.	I will!
Be quiet.	Be quiet!
Your go.	Your go!
Now.	Now!
Give up.	Give up!
Wait.	Wait!

Starting point
Briefly talk about science fiction films the children have seen and the inevitable battles between spaceships.

Read the story
Emphasise the words preceding an exclamation mark to draw attention to it.

Lower order questions
What did Polta look like?
How did Jack and Emily help Polta?
What did the Pintons use as weapons?
What happened to planet Earth?

Higher order questions
Why are exclamation marks important?
How could you use words as weapons?
Can words hurt?
When Emily and Jack were on the spaceship, what could they see?

Points to note
- An exclamation mark is used instead of a full stop.
- Exclamation marks to emphasise what somebody said go inside the speech marks.

Group oral work
Choose one pair of children at a time. Give them a pair of the prepared sheets of words (see Resources). Let each child read their words quietly or in a forceful manner, depending on the punctuation. The rest of the class decides which reader has the full stop and which has the exclamation mark.

Brainstorm words to indicate joy, anger, fear, surprise, shock, pain and so on.

Ask the children to scan their reading books for exclamation marks. Ask them to read out any sentence, word or phrase that precedes an exclamation mark. Remind them to read with expression.

The activity sheets

Sheets 1A, 1B and 1C

1A This is aimed at children who are emergent readers and need support. They should identify some exclamations and write them inside the exclamation marks. Extension – the children use the dots around the page to make a repeating pattern of question marks, exclamation marks and full stops, paying attention to the uniformity of the **?** and **!** size.

1B This is aimed at children who are more confident readers. They should complete four exclamatory phrases (or sentences). Extension – they choose a full stop or exclamation mark to put after the words and phrases in the rocket at the bottom of the sheet.

1C This is aimed at able and more able readers. The children have to choose a minimum of five exclamations and exclamation marks and write them in rocket A, then choose four further exclamation phrases for rocket B. Extension – they complete eight phrases with either **?** or **!**

Sheets 2A, 2B and 2C

2A This is aimed at children who are emergent readers and need support. In each shape there are two phrases. The children have to choose the phrase that is more likely to be an exclamation, then write

it on the line, adding an exclamation mark.
Extension – they complete the rows of exclamation
marks, paying attention to the size.

2B This is aimed at children who are more confident
readers. There are nine exclamation marks behind
the stars. Around the page are isolated words. The
children should find the exclamatory words and
write them in the stars. Extension – the children fill
the flying saucer with as many exclamatory phrases
as possible, remembering to put an exclamation
mark after each one.

2C This is aimed at the able and more able readers.
They select the five phrases that are more likely to
be exclamations and write them in the rocket.
Extension – they write three exciting thoughts,
each followed by an exclamation mark. For
example, *Wow! Help! Yippee! Fantastic! Great!
Look! Oh no!*

Plenary

- Ask what an exclamation mark looks like.
- Ask the children to explain the purpose of an
  exclamation mark.
- Ask the children to read (with expression) some of
  the exclamatory words and phrases they have
  written on their activity sheets.

Cross-curricular activities

Art

Paint a picture of Polta, an intergalactic battle or a
starry sky.

History

Look at the history of flight, including ballooning, the
Wright brothers, jet engines and space travel.

Maths

Compare the distance an A4 sheet will fly when folded
into a darts, with the distance it will fly when
scrunched into a ball.

Polta and the space war

"Duck, you idiots!"

Jack and Emily ducked. A beam of white light whizzed overhead. They looked up and saw a gigantic woman beside them.

She was three metres tall! Her jet black eyes glared out of her pink and orange face. She had long silver hair and she was wearing golden robes. Emily and Jack were standing next to this giant woman, on a narrow platform. In front of them there was a rail. Beyond the rail the black sky was lit up by millions of stars and hundreds of different coloured planets: red, blue, yellow, orange and purple.

"Wow!" exclaimed Jack. "Where are we?"

"You don't know?" asked the giant woman.

The children shook their heads.

"I am POLTA – the space warrior! You are on MY spaceship!"

"Why did you shout at us to duck?" asked Emily.

"We're in the middle of a Pinton exclamation attack," replied Polta.

"A what?" asked Emily.

"Look over there," said Polta, pointing into the dark sky. "See that grey triangle? It's a Pinton Destroyer Spaceship! Pintons want to destroy my spaceship because they want to control space. They use exclamations for weapons!"

"What's an exclamation?" asked Emily.

"Exclamations are fantastic!" cried Polta. "They make ordinary words powerful and strong. 'Go away' becomes 'GO AWAY!'"

She shouted this so loudly the children nearly fell off the platform.

"Sorry," said Polta. "I didn't mean to scare you."

"It's OK," whispered Jack.

"As I was saying," Polta continued, "the Pintons are firing at us. Those powerful bolts of light are exclamations. If they hit us we'll be destroyed!"

Cluttering up the narrow platform were piles of metal rods. They were long and thin with a circle at the end.

"Hey, Emily!" gasped Jack pointing at the rods. "Those are like that thing we found in the chest!"

"What are they?" asked Emily.

Polta picked one up. "They're exclamation marks. When the Pintons fire their next exclamation at us, we'll get them back with one of ours."

Just then a beam of white light headed straight for them. Polta aimed her exclamation mark straight towards the beam of light. She scored a direct hit. Seconds later the words...

We hate you!

appeared in the sky.

"There!" shouted Polta. "I've hit their exclamation mark with mine!"

Suddenly there was a gigantic explosion and the words disappeared.

"Watch out! Here comes another one," shouted Jack.

Another beam of white light was heading straight for them.

"Your turn!" Polta shouted at Jack.

Polta and the space war

Grabbing an exclamation mark from the pile, Jack threw it as hard as he could towards the oncoming light. He scored a direct hit! As the words...

We will completely destroy you, Polta!

blazed across the sky, there was an enormous bang and the words disappeared.

Immediately, another beam of light came flying towards them.

"Your turn, Emily!" yelled Jack.

Emily snatched up an exclamation mark. She flung it with all her might into space and as it reached its target, the words...

You will never beat Pintons!

appeared across the sky. A split second later there was a gigantic explosion and the words disappeared, just like the others.

Emily and Jack grabbed armfuls of exclamation marks. As more enemy white lights came hurtling towards them, they flung their exclamation weapons back in counter-attack. Their aim was fantastic!

The words...

Fighting us is pointless!
We will smash Polta to bits!

lit up the sky.

And, like before, there was a deafening explosion and the words disappeared. The fearsome attacks carried on.

The end is near for you, Polta! Give up!

But Polta, Emily and Jack would not give up. They were fantastic shots. They destroyed every attacking exclamation mark with one of their own.

Suddenly, Polta shouted, "STOP! LOOK! The Pinton Spaceship is flying away. You two have helped me win this space war!"

The three of them looked out into space.

"You used the exclamation marks like experts," smiled Polta.

The children felt proud, but something was worrying Emily.

"Polta," she began, "you know Earth – the planet we come from? I can't see it out there in space. Where is it?"

Polta looked down at Emily and started laughing.

"What's so funny?" asked Jack.

Polta stopped laughing. "A space giant ate planet Earth 60,000 years ago."

"ATE IT?" cried Emily and Jack together.

"Yes," nodded Polta. "He was feeling extremely hungry."

"What about the people, the things ... our school ... what happened to everything?" asked Emily.

But Polta had no time to answer. A loud hissing noise was heard as a blue mist surrounded the children. They were pulled down at an incredible speed. Seconds later they found themselves back in Emily's loft.

Activity sheet 1A

Name _____

✎ Fire the exclamation marks by writing a different exclamation in each one. Choose from these.

Get out!   What's the time?   Wow!
When shall we go?   We'll beat you!   A red bus.
Are you six?   Is it raining?   There's a pig.   Ouch!
The end is near!   The battle begins!   Help!   Stop!
Mind out!

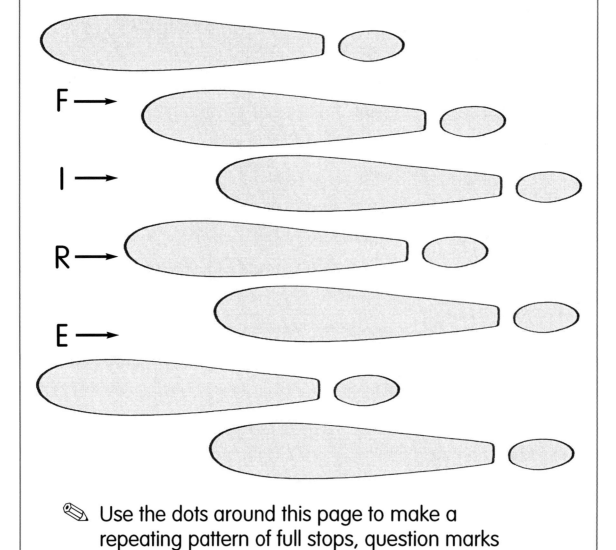

F —→

I —→

R —→

E —→

✎ Use the dots around this page to make a repeating pattern of full stops, question marks and exclamation marks.

✎ The rocket will launch when all the exclamations are complete. The first one has been done for you.

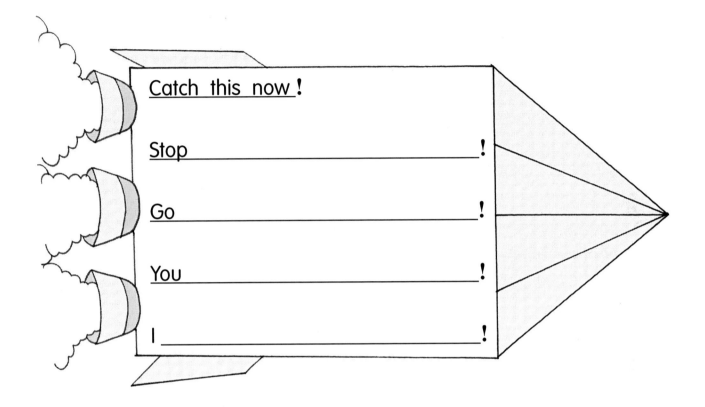

Catch this now!

Stop _____!

Go _____!

You _____!

I _____!

✎ Here are six full stops . . . .
and seven exclamation marks ! ! ! ! ! ! !
Put each one in the correct place in the sentences below.

Polta is very tall	The Moon shines	
The tree is green	Wait for me	Silence
Ouch, that hurt	Earth is a planet	Fire
Mars is the red planet	Watch out	Stop that
I like biscuits	Stop that thief	

Name _____

✎ Five exclamations will fire off rocket A.
Each exclamation MUST have its own exclamation mark.
Choose the exclamation words from this box. Write them in the rocket.

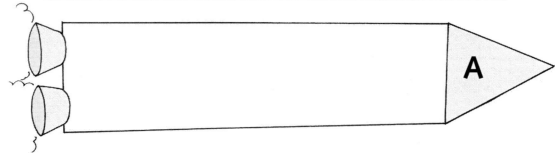

| pink wham bang milk gotcha tadpole ouch |
| fish zap pow aaah crash eek pen |

A

✎ Four exclamations are enough to fire off rocket B.
Remember the exclamation marks!
Choose the exclamation phrases from this box.

Mind out   That's good   That's mine
Catch it   Be quiet   Here's Sammy
Number six   Stop him   Thank you

B

✎ Choose ! or ? to finish these sentences and write them in.

Where is Emily

Go away

Sit down now

Time's up

Ready, steady, go

Who did that

Is it dinner time soon

Why do stars twinkle

Name _____

✎ Make exclamations. Choose the best exclamation from each cloud. Write it out and don't forget the exclamation mark. The first one has been done for you.

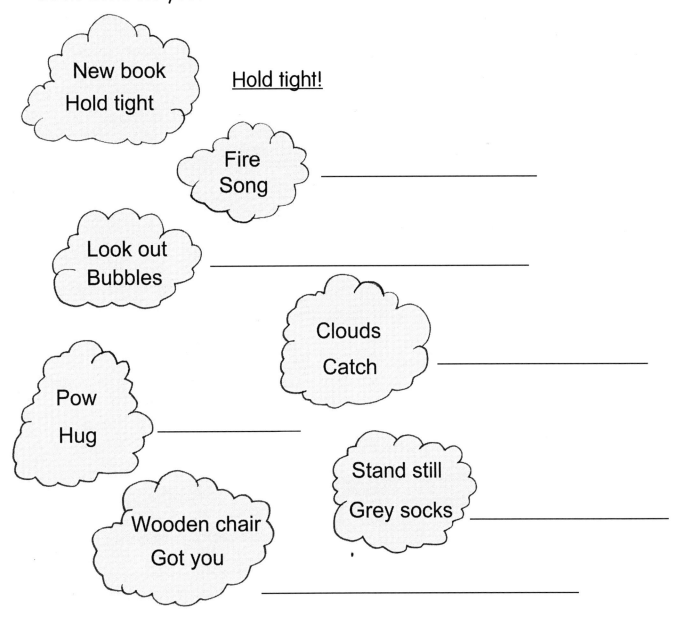

New book
Hold tight

Hold tight!

Fire
Song

_____

Look out
Bubbles

_____

Clouds
Catch

_____

Pow
Hug

_____

Stand still
Grey socks

_____

Wooden chair
Got you

_____

✎ Complete this row of exclamation marks.

✎ Make a row of ten exclamation marks.

_____

✎ Write exclamations in the stars to fire the exclamation marks at the enemy spaceship.

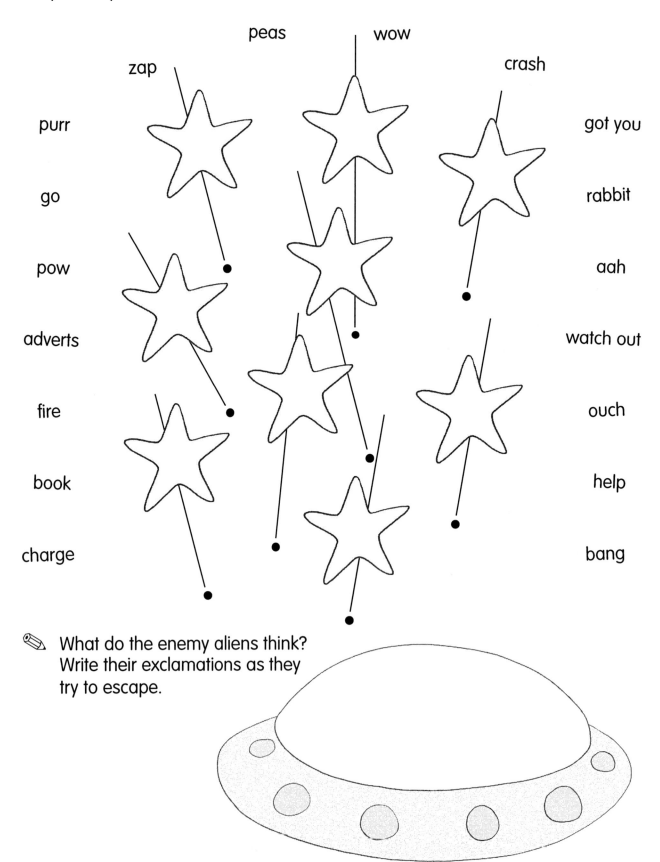

peas   wow

zap   crash

purr   got you

go   rabbit

pow   aah

adverts   watch out

fire   ouch

book   help

charge   bang

✎ What do the enemy aliens think?
Write their exclamations as they
try to escape.

Name _____

✎ Write the exclamation phrases in the rocket to shoot it through the clouds. Write the other phrases in the clouds. Don't forget the exclamation marks!

Go away   Blue shoes   That's amazing

You're finished   That's brilliant   Biscuit crumbs

Wet socks   Stop that   Soft breezes   Happy dreams

✎ How would you feel if you were in a rocket racing into space?

Write three thoughts here.

_____   _____   _____

Speech marks

Intended learning
- To know that words actually spoken (direct speech) are contained within speech marks.

Preparation and resources
- On the board draw large opening and closing speech marks, with enough space to write four or five words between them. (Use double speech marks – both single and double are correct. As the activity sheets use double speech marks it is best to use them in the lesson to avoid confusion. You can explain to the children that both are correct.)
- Write each of the phrases below on a separate slip of paper.

  I went to the dentist.

  I can swim.

  He's been to Scotland.

  There's a wasp.

  They keep chickens.

  Tom will be ten on Monday.

  My uncle supports Liverpool.

  I stayed up late.

Starting point
One by one, ask the children simple questions. For example:

How old are you?

What is the date?

Which month is this?

Who is sitting near you?

What's the name of the teacher next door?

Write the replies between the speech marks on the board, emphasising the point that only *spoken words* go between the speech marks.

Read the story
Emphasise direct speech by reading the spoken words at an increased volume.

Lower order questions
What did Emily and Jack use to catch words?
What did Emily and Jack catch on Noisy Beach?
Where did Emily and Jack take all the words?
Was the curse broken?
Could the people speak again?

Higher order questions
How do speech marks help when we read?
How are fishing hooks and speech marks similar?
What do people mean when they say, "I'm sorry. I didn't catch that."?
Does the word 'said' always follow speech marks?

Points to note
- There are different ways of writing speech marks; double (" ") and single (' ').
- In print, the basic comma shape is sometimes rotated or inverted.
- Speech marks always go at the same height as the tops of capital letters.

Group oral work
Ask pairs of children to demonstrate direct speech, using the prepared slips of paper.

Billy (reads): *I went to the dentist.*
Sally: *Billy said, "I went to the dentist."*
Whole class: *Billy said, "I went to the dentist."*

Read out the 'answers' below. For each one ask the children to make up a question.
ten; tomorrow; apples; yellow; three-nil; trainers; spiders; 50p; swimming; Sanjay; the hall; by coach; a Gameboy; 8:30

The activity sheets

Sheets 1A, 1B and 1C

1A This is aimed at children who are emergent readers and need support. They should write the spoken words (direct speech) inside the speech marks. Remind them that the first spoken word must *always* begin with a capital letter. Extension – the children put speech marks round each of the eight words, taking care with the position of the speech marks. Finally, they make a sentence using one of the eight words.

1B This is aimed at children who are more confident readers. They should put the spoken words (direct speech) inside the speech marks. Note that the first spoken word *must* begin with a capital letter. Extension – the children have to write two sentences using speech marks.

1C This is aimed at able and more able readers. They have to fit the questions and exclamations into the appropriate gaps. Remind them that each question or exclamation *must* begin with a capital letter. Extension – the six sentences contain direct speech but the speech marks are missing. The children should add speech marks round the spoken words, paying close attention to the position of the speech marks.

Sheets 2A, 2B and 2C

2A This is aimed at children who are emergent readers and need support. There are two buckets, each containing direct speech. The children have to put speech marks round each of the spoken phrases in the buckets, taking care with the position of the speech marks. Extension – the children should read the ten sentences, then copy out the three that contain a sea creature. They then draw a picture of a sea creature.

2B This is aimed at children who are more confident readers. There are two buckets. One contains questions; the other contains answers. The children should match the answers to the questions, remembering to add speech marks when writing the answers. Extension – they have to write two sentences, each containing direct speech.

2C This is aimed at able and more able readers. The eight sentences each contain direct speech. The children write four direct speech phrases in each bucket. Extension – the children should write three sentences, each including their teacher's direct speech.

Plenary

- Ask the children the following questions:

  - What do speech marks look like?
  - Where do speech marks go?
  - Which words go in between speech marks?
  - What is important about the first word of direct speech? (It starts with a capital letter.)

- Ask some of the children to read out the original sentences they wrote for extension activities 1A, 1B, 2B and 2C.

Cross-curricular activities

Physical education

Play O'Grady (or Simon) Says, but instead say, "Speech marks say…" Hook both index and middle fingers in the air to indicate speech marks each time you say "Speech marks say…"

Science

Put two or three coins at the bottom of a bucket of water. Drop other coins into the water and record how many times a 'hit' is made onto the original coins. The story is about catching words – aiming for (targeting) spoken words. This science experiment is about aiming for a target (in this instance a coin). Dropping one coin onto another through the air will pull it straight down and the coin will inevitably hit the target. If you drop a coin through water, the water will cause the coin to 'plane' and the chances of a direct hit will be considerably reduced.

The purpose of the experiment is to focus the children's minds on what they want to 'catch'. The experiment is to heighten children's awareness of targeting something specific. In relating this to the story and to punctuation, the children will become more aware of 'targeting' something in their script.

The children will be fascinated by not scoring many hits with the coins but scoring direct hits with speech marks round spoken words.

PSHE

Talk about water safety on and around rivers, lakes, canals, swimming pools and the sea.

Reflect on the power of water, especially floods and the catastrophic tsunami of December 2004.

Diving in the deep

Emily and Jack were in the loft.

Emily reached for a tiny metal fishing hook in the wooden chest.

"Look at this," she whispered.

"Leave it," said Jack. "We're going out soon."

But it was too late.

Emily had already touched the hook and they were immediately surrounded by a blue mist and being pulled upwards at an incredible speed.

They found themselves deep under water, standing on the seabed.

They were both wearing diving gear.

Everywhere Emily and Jack looked, they saw beautiful fish and sea horses. There were also thousands of fishing hooks lying on the sand, exactly like the one Emily had picked up from the chest in the loft.

"I wondered when you two were going to turn up," said a friendly-looking diver.

"Why are we here?" asked Emily.

"I need you to collect fishing hooks," replied the diver.

Emily and Jack swam around collecting hooks. After fifteen minutes they had collected loads of them.

"Now follow me," shouted the diver.

Three ropes suddenly appeared. The diver grabbed one and was pulled up to the surface. Emily and Jack caught the other ropes and felt themselves being hauled up...

Diving in the deep

to a sandy beach. The diver was still in his diving gear but mysteriously Emily and Jack were now in shorts and T-shirts.

There was noise everywhere. Parents were chatting, children were shouting, babies were gurgling.

Every time anyone said something, Emily and Jack could see the words floating out of their mouth.

"This is Noisy Beach," explained the diver. "Use the hooks to catch things people say – their speech. Emily, you put a hook at the beginning of speech and Jack, you put a hook at the end."

"Hey, that's like speech marks!" said Jack.

"Exactly!" smiled the diver. "And the best part is that no one can see you! I want every speech you catch to be dropped in my basket here."

"But why do we need to catch speech?" asked Emily.

"I promise I'll tell you later," winked the diver.

Emily and Jack dashed around the beach excitedly.

Here's a towel, said a mother to her son.

Emily and Jack watched the words floating in the air. Emily put a hook at the beginning of the speech and Jack put a hook at the end.

Here's a towel.

So it looked like this:

"Here's a towel.**"**

They ran and dropped it into the diver's bucket.

They carried on along the beach, catching speech with their hooks.

Diving in the deep

"Do you want an ice cream?"

"I love this sunny weather."

"Shall we have a barbecue tonight?"

When they'd dropped lots of speech into the diver's bucket he told them to stop.

He clicked his fingers and suddenly all three of them were on another beach. But this one was completely different from Noisy Beach. It was silent except for the gentle sound of waves.

There were crowds of people but no one was saying anything at all.

"Welcome to Silent Beach," said the diver.

"Why is it called that?" asked Emily.

"Over a hundred years ago," the diver explained, "the people on this beach stopped pirates from stealing their gold and treasures. In revenge the pirates put a curse on them. They took away the islanders' power of speech! So it became known as 'Silent Beach'. No one has spoken here for a hundred years. But you two can return their power of speech."

"How?" asked Jack.

"Take this bucket, run along the beach and throw the phrases with their speech marks high into the air. With hundreds of bits of speech floating around, the pirates' curse will be broken."

Emily and Jack raced off and after a few minutes they had emptied the bucket of speech. As they ran past a palm tree back to the diver they suddenly heard a boy calling to his mother.

"Mum!"

His mother stared at him with amazement.

"You spoke!" she cried.

"So did you!" shouted the boy.

Suddenly all around them people started speaking and laughing and cheering.

"The curse is broken!" someone yelled.
"We can speak again!"

"Congratulations!" smiled the diver, walking to meet Emily and Jack.

"You've done brilliantly. From now on, every time you write about someone saying something, think of those fishing hooks. That way you'll always remember to use speech marks for speech."

"We will," replied Emily and Jack.

"Race you through the waterfall, Jack," laughed Emily.

As they raced into the misty blue spray, they were pulled downwards at an incredible speed.

They heard Emily's mum calling.

"Hurry up, you two! We're going to that new diving pool in five minutes," she shouted.

Name _____

✎ These words have been caught by fishing hooks.
Put each word into a sentence.

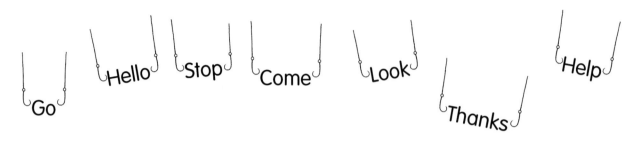

" _____," said Emily.

" _____," Emily said.

" _____," Emily said.

" _____," Emily said.

Jack said, " _____."

He said, " _____."

He whispered, " _____."

Jack said, " _____."

✎ Carefully put speech marks round each of the words below.

Yes.   No.   Me.   Today.   Friday.   Yellow.   Hooks.   Gold.

✎ Now make your own sentence using one of the words.

_____

Name _____

✎ Look at the words Emily and Jack are leaving on Silent Beach.
Use the words to complete the sentences.

Here you are

Come in

Look

Stop

I won

Here I am

Can we play?

Can we go?

Goo-goo

" _____," said a girl.

" _____," laughed a boy.

" _____" the twins asked.

" _____," cooed the baby.

" _____," said a man.

" _____," said the lifeguard.

" _____" said the children.

" _____," whispered a granny.

" _____," someone's mum said.

✎ Write two things that Emily and Jack might say about the sea.
Remember to use speech marks.

_____

_____

Name _____

 Emily and Jack have caught so many words.
Some of the words are for shouting and some are for asking questions.
Write in the correct words to complete each sentence.

Got you!   Who did that?

Mind that!   Where are you?

Get out!

When must we go?

Why me?

Jump now!

Jack asked, "_____."

"_____" asked Jack.

"_____" he asked.

Jack asked, "_____"

"_____" yelled Emily.

"_____" Emily shouted.

Emily yelled, "_____"

She shouted, "_____"

Put speech marks round Emily and Jack's spoken words.

Jack asked, Have you seen Emily?

Is that a sea horse? Jack asked.

Jack said, I'm going for a swim.

Emily said, This beach is too hot for me.

Watch out! shouted Emily.

Can't catch me, laughed Emily.

Name _____

✎ Look at the words in Jack and Emily's buckets.

   Put speech marks round each set of spoken words.

There's an octopus.

Can I have a go?

That's fantastic!

I like that!

Quick, hide!

Will you come?

Here's a crab.

Look, a starfish.

Stop splashing!

That stinks!

✎ Write down the three sentences that have a sea creature in them.

1. _____

2. _____

3. _____

✎ Draw a picture of a sea creature on the back of this sheet.

Name _____

Emily and Jack have collected words in their buckets.

Emily has caught questions. Jack has caught answers.

"Is your bucket full?"
"Where shall we go?"
"Can crabs pinch?"
"What is the time?"

"Let's go home."
"Big crabs pinch hard!"
"It's ten o'clock."
"Full to the top."

Put the questions and answers in the right places.

Emily asked, "Can _____

       Jack replied, _____

She asked, "Is _____

       Jack said, _____

Emily asked, "Where _____

       Jack answered, _____

Emily asked, _____

       Jack answered, _____

 What would <u>an old person</u> say on the beach?

_____

What would <u>you</u> say on the beach?

_____

Name _____

 The people at Noisy Beach are shouting and yelling.
Help Emily and Jack catch four spoken phrases each.
Write them in the buckets.

The girl shrieked, "Mind that crab!"   "I'm going for a swim," said Ben.

"What's that creature?" asked Ali.   "I've lost my goggles," moaned Jo.

Jake shouted, "I've found a pound!"   "There's a red balloon," said Molly.

"Sun hats for sale!" yelled the man.   "Want an ice cream?" asked a boy.

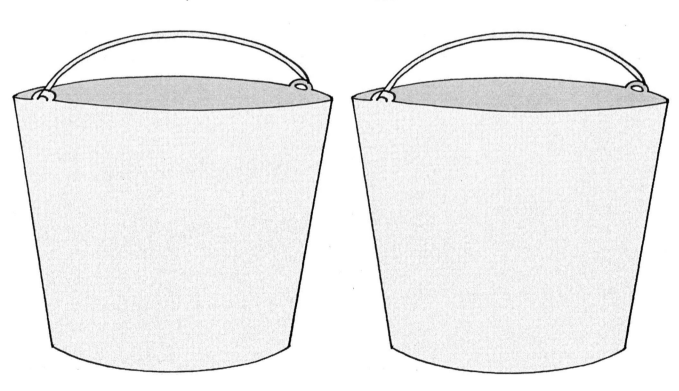

 Write three things your teacher has said today.

1. My teacher said, " _____."

2. _____

3. _____

Question words

Intended learning
- To know and use a range of question words.
- To recognise that these words at the beginning of a sentence mean that the sentence is a question.

Preparation and resources
- On the board write:

  This _is_ the winner.
  I _can_ go out to play.
  The old dragon _did_ breathe fire.
  The dragon _was_ weeping.

Starting point
Ask the class to look at the four sentences on the board. Turn them into questions by saying the underlined word first.

Brainstorm question words (will, how, why, where, is, when, have, what, who, can, which, did) and write them on the board.

Read the story
Before you begin, explain these words: plaque, engraved, decades.

Exaggerate all the question words you come across as you read the story.

Lower order questions
Where were Emily and Jack?
What could they see from the window?
What did they throw from the window?
What did the beast need to eat?

Higher order questions
What is a question?
What are question words used for?
What difference does it make if you use the word 'please' in a question?
Why do some people ask the same question over and over again?

Points to note
- Emphasise that asking questions is a very positive thing to do. Explain that scientists and explorers constantly ask questions and then investigate to try and find answers.

- A sentence that asks a question must have a question mark at the end.

Group oral work
Invite some children to select some of the words generated in the brainstorm and turn them into questions.

The activity sheets

Sheets 1A, 1B and 1C
1A This is aimed at children who are emergent readers and need support. They should pick out six different question words from a selection on the wall and write them on the beast's scales. Extension – the children have to select the correct question words to complete each of four questions.

1B This is aimed at children who are more confident readers. There are seven incomplete questions. The children have to select a word from the wall of question words to complete each question. Extension – the children should write three questions to ask a dragon. Remind them to put a question mark at the end.

1C This is aimed at able and more able readers. There are six questions, each with the wrong question word at the beginning. The children have to think of a better question word and write it on the line. Extension – the children should compose a question to go with each of four answers.

Sheets 2A, 2B and 2C
2A This is aimed at children who are emergent readers and need support. The words of six questions have been muddled up. The children should sort out and rewrite each question, starting with a question word with a capital letter. Extension – the letters of five question words have been muddled up. The children have to sort out the letters and write the question words.

2B This is aimed at children who are more confident readers. There are six muddled up questions. The children should find the question word in each and rewrite the sentence in order, using an initial capital letter for the question word. Remind them to put a question mark at the end. Extension – ten question words have joined together to make a line of letters. The children have to separate the words by drawing lines between them, then choose three of the words and use them to write three questions.

2C This is aimed at able and more able readers. There are question words on the flag and muddled words in the tower. The children should choose a word from the flag then sort out the muddled words to make a question. Extension – the children have to write four questions that a dragon might ask.

Plenary

• Ask the children to think about what questions they need to answer when writing an invitation. (*What* is happening? *Where* is it happening? *When* is it happening? And so on.)

• How many question words can the children remember?

• If there's a question word at the beginning of a sentence, what is ALWAYS at the end?

• Ask children to read out the sentences written for the extension activities on sheets 1B, 1C and 2C.

Cross-curricular activities

Literature

Brainstorm other stories in which castles are featured: Rumpelstiltskin, Jack and the Beanstalk, Cinderella, The Hunchback of Notre Dame, Puss in Boots, The Princess and the Pea, Beauty and the Beast, Robin Hood (Nottingham Castle) and Sleeping Beauty.

Ask the children questions such as:
• What's good about living in a castle?
• What's not good about living in a castle?
• Are castles secure places to hold people prisoner?
• Would it be difficult to escape from a castle?

There is an excellent website (www.castlexplorer.co.uk).

Design and technology

Make some castles and towers using cereal or washing powder boxes. Stick squares of card to the top of the box to represent castellations. Paint the box to represent a stone built tower. Paint a portcullis. Paint small slit windows. Construct a drawbridge by fixing (with tape) a square of card to the base of the box. The card, when lifted up, should cover the portcullis.

Draw an outline of a large dragon. Ask the children to make lots of scales (postcard size) on green, brown and orange paper. On each scale they write a question on one side and an answer on the reverse, such as 'What day comes after Monday?' 'Tuesday.' And 'Are dragons real?' 'Yes, in story books!' The children stick their scales in the outline of the dragon.

History and Geography

What was the purpose of a keep in a castle?
Find a list of castles, using books, encyclopedias and the internet.

On a map of the UK, show the children places where there are castles: The Tower of London, Windsor Castle, Leeds Castle in Kent, Nottingham Castle, Caernarvon Castle, Cardiff Castle, Carisbrooke Castle (Isle of Wight).

Ask the children the following questions:
• Why are the castles built where they are? (Defense/security)
• Who would have lived in castles? (Royalty – knights – court.)
• Does anyone live in castles nowadays? (Royalty)
• How do we keep our own homes safe? (Locks and keys.)
• How is school kept safe? (Locks and CCTV.)

Escape from the tower

"What is **that**?" whispered Emily.

Emily and Jack were in a square room at the top of a tower. They were peering through a narrow window. In a courtyard down below, a horse was tied to a post. Next to it lay a giant beast, a bit like a dragon but silver with a furry back.

"I've never seen anything like it," said Jack. "It doesn't look scary, just sad."

"If the beast isn't scary, let's go!" said Jack. He stepped out of the window onto a long ladder that stretched down to the courtyard. But as soon as he started to climb down, the beast stood up and roared.

Jack dived back into the room, slamming the window shut.

"We were wrong about it not being scary!" gasped Emily.

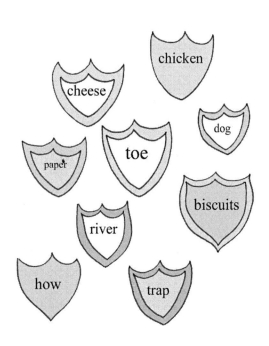

Looking round the room, Jack said, "This must have something to do with that knife you took from the chest in the loft, Emily."

Emily looked at the rusty old knife. Then she looked at the walls of the room, which were covered with metal plaques. Each plaque had a single word engraved on it.

"Maybe the knife is connected to the words on the wall. Read some out, Jack."

He read: *paper, dog, chicken, river, cheese, trap, how, biscuits, toe...*

"I've got it!" said Emily, excitedly. "The beast is hungry. Let's use the knife to cut off the food words. The beast will eat them and fall asleep and then we can escape on that horse."

"Great idea!" nodded Jack.

"Here, catch!" called Emily, cutting the *eggs* plaque off the wall and tossing it to Jack.

He opened the window and threw it into the courtyard.

They watched. The beast sniffed it, then walked away sadly.

"No good," sighed Jack.

"Of course!" said Emily. "Beasts eat living things, not biscuits!"

She cut off *sparrow*, *slug* and *lizard*. Jack threw them into the courtyard. The beast sniffed them, then kicked them away and started crying huge silver tears.

"Why don't you tell us what you want?" Jack shouted down. But he leant too far over the edge and toppled out.

"Aaaaaaaaaaahhhhhhhhhhhhhh!" he yelled.

Luckily Emily was right behind him and grabbed his leg. For a few seconds Jack dangled upside down, the beast gazing up at him.

Using all her strength, Emily dragged him back in.

"Thanks," gasped Jack. "You saved my life but we're still no closer to escaping."

Escape from the tower

"How about throwing loads and loads of plaques to scare it away," Emily suggested. "What d'you think?"

"Let's go for it," agreed Jack.

Emily prised off: *pen, fire, river, where, arrow, biscuits, brush, plate.*

Jack hurled them out but this time stayed well away from the edge.

As they hit the ground the beast sprang at one and gobbled it up.

"It ate one!" yelled Jack.

"Which one?" shouted Emily.

"*Where*," called Jack.

"That's it," beamed Emily. "It wants the words beginning with 'w'."

She cut down *whip, wheel, wheat* and *white*.
Jack threw them down. The beast glanced at them and groaned.

"No good!" stamped Jack in disappointment.

"WAIT!" Emily cried. "*Where* is a QUESTION WORD. Perhaps it wants question words."

She quickly cut down *who, what, why, which, how, when* and *can*. As soon as Jack dropped the words out, the beast leapt onto them, devouring them greedily.

"Look, Emily, the beast is changing," cried Jack.

Emily hurried over. They watched as the beast grew smaller and smaller. In less than a minute it had become a knight in silver armour.

"Thank you, my friends," the knight called out. "A wicked wizard put a curse on me when I asked him too many questions. He turned me into a beast. He said I'd only become myself again if I ate all the question words from this tower. I've been waiting decades for someone to cut those words off and feed them to me."

The knight then untied the horse and leapt into the saddle.

"Farewell!" he called. "Thank you again! Now I'm going after that wizard!"

He galloped away in a swirl of dust.

"Come on," said Emily. "Let's get down that ladder."

As they began clattering down the ladder a blue mist surrounded them.

Moments later it cleared away and they found themselves on Emily's loft ladder.

"Hey, you two!" called Emily's mum from downstairs. "Take it easy climbing down that ladder. It sounds like you're running away from some sort of fearsome beast!"

Name _____

✎ To escape from the tower, Jack and Emily must feed question words to the hungry beast.

Find six question words and write them on the beast's back.

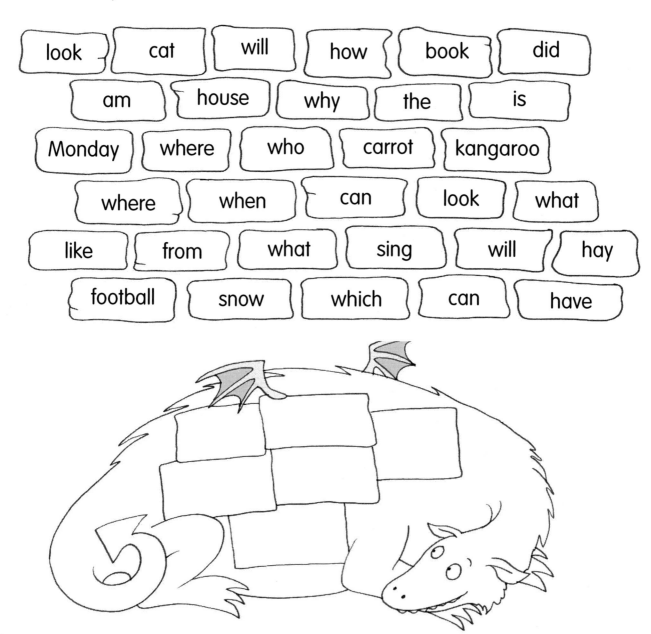

look	cat	will	how	book	did
am	house	why	the	is
Monday	where	who	carrot	kangaroo
where	when	can	look	what
like	from	what	sing	will	hay
football	snow	which	can	have

✎ Find question words on the wall to complete these sentences.

1. _____ is my hat?

2. _____ is the time?

3. _____ has that broken?

4. _____ I colour the beast?

Name _____

✎ Complete the sentences using question words, to make the beast go away.

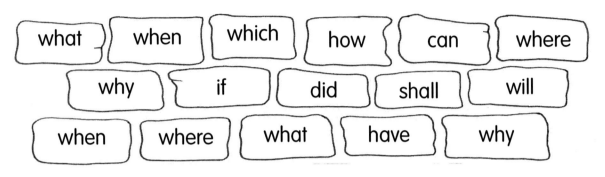

" _____ do you want?" asked Jack.

" _____ do dragons live?" Emily asked.

" _____ it breathe fire?" Jack asked.

" _____ do you say sorry?" she asked.

" _____ word shall I choose?" thought Emily.

" _____ can we escape?" whispered Jack.

" _____ you see a way out?" asked Emily.

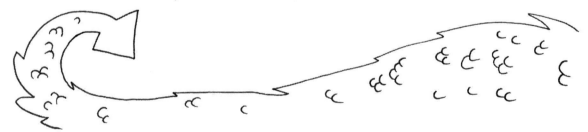

✎ Write three questions you would ask a dragon.

1. _____

2. _____

3. _____

✎ Colour the dragon's tail.

Name _____

✎ The dragon has put the wrong question word into each question.

Write the correct word instead.

Will do dragons stink?

_____ do dragons stink?

Which did that happen?

_____ did that happen?

What you see anything?

_____ you see anything?

Can does the match start?

_____ does the match start?

Will shall we do?

_____ shall we do?

Can is the dragon looking?

_____ is the dragon looking?

✎ Write questions for these answers.

1. _____ Two-nil.

2. _____ Friday.

3. _____ 10p.

4. _____ It's yellow.

Name _____

✎ The sentences in each room of the tower are muddled up.
Sort the words into order and throw them out of the tower.

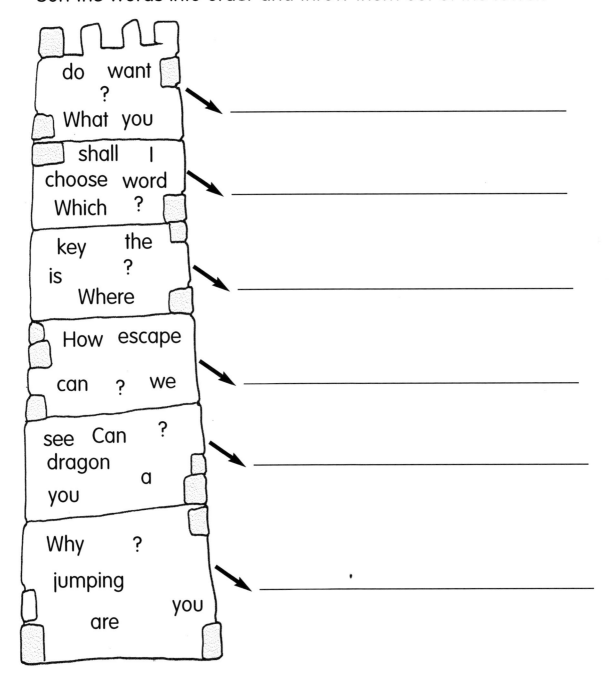

do   want   ?
What   you
_____

shall   I
choose   word
Which   ?
_____

key   the
is   ?
Where
_____

How   escape
can   ?   we
_____

see   Can   ?
dragon   a
you
_____

Why   ?
jumping
you
are
_____

✎ Sort out these muddled question words.

hwy   htaw   wheer   nac   woh

_____   _____   _____   _____   _____

Name _____

✎ The sentences in each room of the tower are muddled up.
Sort them out and add a question mark.

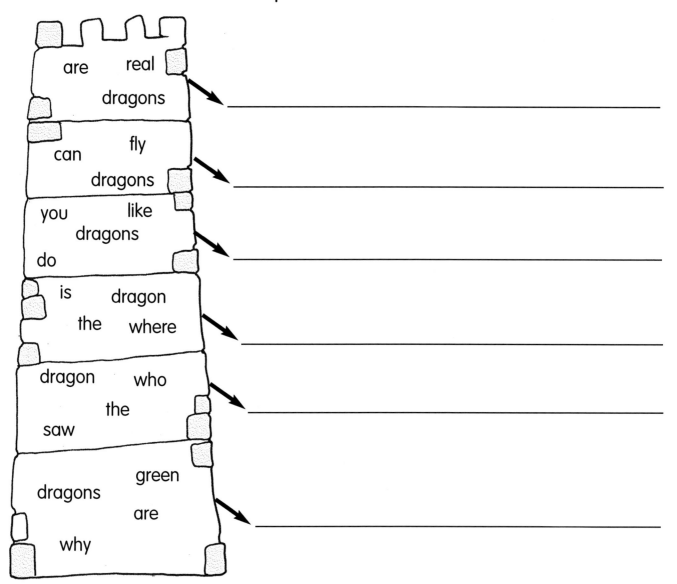

are   real
dragons   _____

can   fly
dragons   _____

you   like
dragons   _____
do

is   dragon
the   where   _____

dragon   who
the   _____
saw

green
dragons   _____
are
why

✎ Separate the question words by drawing lines between them.

howwhycanwillwherehavewhichwhatwouldwhen

Choose three words and write your own questions.

1. _____

2. _____

3. _____

Name _____

✎ Help Emily and Jack make questions. Sort out the muddled words
in each room and add a question word from the flag.

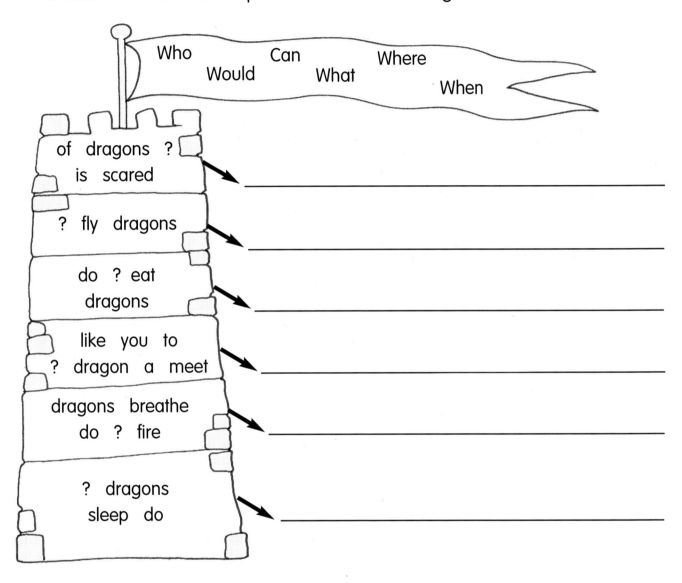

Who   Can   Where
    Would   What
                          When

of dragons ?
    is scared   _____

? fly dragons   _____

do ? eat
    dragons   _____

like you to
? dragon a meet   _____

dragons breathe
    do ? fire   _____

? dragons
    sleep do   _____

✎ Write four questions a dragon would ask you!

1. _____

2. _____

3. _____

4. _____

Commas

Intended learning

- To know that commas are used when writing a list.
- To be aware that commas and speech marks often go together.

Preparation and resources

- Write the following on the board:

   comma 　　　　　　　　 **,**

   banquet　　　　　　 *menu*

- A variety of reading books showing direct speech.

Starting point

Tell the children a comma is a brief pause between items in a list and is used instead of the word 'and'.

Show that inside a sentence with direct speech there is usually a comma before the speech marks. For example:

He opened the door and said, "Hello."
Mum shouted, "Stop that!"
Teacher whispered, "Well done."
Joe called, "See you!"
He said, "That's half price today."

The children could find sentences with direct speech from their reading books and identify the comma that precedes direct speech.

Read the story

Explain the words 'banquet' and 'menu' before reading the story.

Ask children their understanding of 'banquet'. (A grand and formal meal. People are invited, as opposed to dining in a restaurant/cafe.) How does a banquet differ from a packed lunch? How does a banquet differ from tea time at home?

Ask children their understanding of 'menu'. (A list of options – perhaps food choices – options on the computer screen.)

Lower order questions

List five colours.
List five fruits.
List five animals.
List five girls' names.
List five boys' names.

Ask the children to draw a comma in the air between each word in the lists.

Higher order questions

Are commas important?
What is a menu?
(Talk about food and computer menus.)
How do punctuation marks help the reader?
When you are reading, what do you do when you see a comma in a sentence?

Points to note

- Stress that it is very important to make commas sit on the line. Other punctuation marks use the same shaped mark in different positions, so commas that wander off the line could muddle the reader.

Group oral work

Ask the children to look in the collection of reading books and find sentences with direct speech. Read the sentences and discuss the use of commas with direct speech marks. Write on the board:

1. *Jack said, "Look in here."*

   "Look in here," said Jack.

2. *He whispered "Come here."*

   "Come here　" he whispered.

In example 2 where should the commas be?

The activity sheets

Sheets 1A, 1B and 1C

1A This sheet is aimed at children who are emergent readers and need support. A number of commas are missing from each sentence. The children insert the missing commas in the correct places. Extension – the children form commas, taking care with the precise position of the comma.

1B This sheet is aimed at more confident readers. Each of six sentences contains a list but no commas. The children are asked to insert commas in the correct places. Extension – the children rewrite a food list, adding spaces and commas, then make their own list of foods they like in sandwiches.

1C This sheet is for the able and more able children. The children insert the missing commas into eight sentences. Extension – the children make a list of mini-beasts and words that begin with 'm'.

Commas

Sheets 2A, 2B and 2C

2A This sheet is aimed at children who are emergent readers and need support. A selection of foods is listed on a menu board. The children complete two sentences, using items from the board, make a list of words beginning with C and make a list of five letter words. Extension – draw a main meal and a pudding. Write a list of items in each.

2B This sheet is aimed at more confident readers. The children separate the words in five lists with spaces and commas. Extension – design an invitation card to a banquet, including a list of foods to be served.

2C This sheet is for the able and more able children in the class. The children insert commas in six sentences. Extension – the children make two lists; one of foods they don't like, the other of things a wizard would put in a potion.

Plenary

- Ask children to describe what a comma looks like.
- Ask children to explain why the position of a comma on the line is important.
- Ask children to explain when and where a comma is used.
- Ask children to read out their activity sheet sentences. Remind them to hesitate slightly at commas.

Cross-curricular activities

Art

Ask children to bring photos of themselves to school. Blow the photos up to life size on the photocopier. Let the children stick curled strips of paper to the photocopies so it looks as though they are wearing wigs.

Maths

Make a chart showing preferred fruit. Explore which is the most popular fruit, the least popular fruit, how many people like strawberries, oranges and kiwis. How many MORE people like grapes than bananas? How many FEWER people like oranges than apples?

Make two charts with columns divided into days of the week. One is for fresh fruit, the other for dried fruit. Children who have eaten fresh fruit at lunch time write their name on the relevant chart. Those who have eaten dried fruit write on the relevant chart.

Maths work from the charts could include:
- How many children ate fresh fruit on Wednesday?
- How many children ate dried fruit on Friday?
- On which days did more children eat fresh fruit?
- On which days did fewer children eat fresh fruit?
- Who ate fresh fruit every day?

Science

Ask the children what healthy food is. List healthy food on the board, thus reinforcing the use of the comma by listing the food in sentences:
We like carrots, apples, rice and cucumber.
We like cheese, grapes, fish fingers, peas and sultanas.

Ask the children to make a list of the healthy foods they would include in their packed lunch box.

Fold a sheet of A4 paper in half. The top half represents the lid of the packed lunch box. The children design the lid and write their name prominently on it. Lift the lid to reveal the 'inside' of the box. The children could draw segments in the box and write in each segment healthy foods they like to eat.

The Queen's banquet

Emily and Jack were looking inside the chest in the loft.

"Look at that funny old wig!" laughed Jack.

As soon as Jack touched it, he and Emily were surrounded by the blue mist and felt themselves being pulled upwards at an incredible speed.

As the mist cleared they found themselves standing in an enormous dining room. At the far side of the room was a huge wooden dining table.

There were servants everywhere. They were carrying trays laden with food, holding silver jugs and setting down cutlery on the massive table.

"You two!" a voice shouted.

Emily and Jack looked round. A tall, angry-looking man came striding towards them.

"The Queen's banquet starts in an hour!" he boomed.

"What's a banquet?" Jack whispered to Emily.

"A sort of giant feast, I think," Emily replied.

"Right," said the man, pointing at Jack. "You, boy, are needed to help prepare the royal wigs. Hurry up!"

Jack nodded and hurried towards a sign that said 'Palace Wig Chamber'.

"And you," he said, looking at Emily. "You're going to write out the menu for today's banquet. Here's the list of food and drink."

He threw Emily a piece of paper and two long sticks of white chalk.

The Queen's banquet

Emily spotted a large blackboard standing next to the table.

"Well, what are you waiting for?" barked the man.

Emily ran over to the blackboard.

"Yuk!" she thought to herself, looking at the list. "Frogs' legs, apples and earwigs!"

She took a piece of chalk and started writing on the board.

Almost at once, the tall man appeared beside her. "Is that all you've written?" he cried. "GET ON WITH IT! THE QUEEN AND HER GUESTS WILL BE HERE VERY SOON!"

Meanwhile, Jack was in the PALACE Wig Chamber.

Lined up on a long table were hundreds of wigs.

A short, nervous-looking woman scurried in.

"Thank goodness you're here!" she gasped.

"What am I supposed to do with these?" frowned Jack.

"Prepare them like this," she whispered, as she quickly combed and powdered a wig and carefully trimmed any stray wisps – snip, snip, snip.

"And don't forget to check the wigs for mice," she added.

Jack wondered, "Is she joking, or what?"

He started the job.

The long curly wigs were disgusting. They smelled awful, like sweaty trainers and dirty socks.

The Queen's banquet

Lots of loose curls were falling off the wigs onto the floor.

"Careful! Don't drop any more curls on the floor!" cried the woman at him, as she hurried out of the room.

Meanwhile, back in the dining room, Emily was struggling. It was fine when she wrote food and drink words but whenever she tried to write a comma, the chalk wouldn't do it.

"But I need commas," Emily thought. "When you write a list you have to put a comma between each word."

The tall man appeared again.

"What on earth are you doing?" he yelled. "There are no commas in your lists!"

"I'm trying!" Emily replied. "But…"

"I don't want to hear 'buts'," he shouted. "I'll be back in ten minutes and I want to see those commas."

Emily was stuck. The chalk simply would not write commas. She ran quietly across the room and slipped into the Palace Wig Chamber.

Jack was busy powdering wigs. There were hundreds of curls lying on the floor.

"Jack!" Emily called urgently. "I need your help! The chalk I'm using won't write commas. I must have commas for lists."

"I'm in trouble too!" Jack replied. "Look at all the curls on the floor."

"Hey!" yelled Emily. "I've got an idea that will help the two of us!"

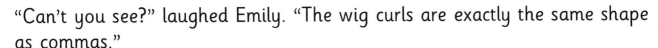
Quickly, she started picking up the wig curls. Jack did the same. Soon the floor was clean and they both had an armful of wig curls.

"Follow me!" said Emily.

They dashed across the dining room to the blackboard.

Emily snatched a curl and put it on the board. It stuck perfectly.

"What are you doing?" hissed Jack.

"Can't you see?" laughed Emily. "The wig curls are exactly the same shape as commas."

She grabbed more curls and stuck them between the food words. At last her menu lists were starting to look good.

At that moment, the tall man walked over to them.

"What are you doing out here?" he shouted at Jack. "You're supposed to be working on the wigs!"

Suddenly, Emily and Jack were surrounded by blue mist and found themselves being pulled downwards at an incredible speed.

They found themselves back in the loft and hurried downstairs.

"What's happened to your hair?" Emily's mum asked them. "You look like you've been wearing wigs!"

Name _____

✎ The commas are missing from the sentences below.
Jack and Emily have put the right number of curls in the box next to each sentence. Put them in the sentences.

,

I like chips pizza and peas.

, , ,

Weekdays are Monday Tuesday Wednesday Thursday and Friday.

, , ,

Emily Jack Navjit Mohammed and Ali are in the team.

, ,

They have maths English history and art every Monday.

,

Spiderman Batman and Peter Pan can all fly.

✎ Make these full stops into commas.

. . . .

✎ Make your own row of commas.

_____

Name _____

✎ Put the curly commas in the correct places in each sentence.

In the kitchen there were wigs mice pots and pans.

The dusty wig was brown grey and white.

Cats cars commas and curls all begin with the same letter.

There were eggs bananas cakes grapes and buns to eat.

Sometimes the scissors went snip snip snip snip on their own!

There were pots pans jugs and dishes piled on a table.

✎ Rewrite the food words with spaces and commas.

There were **b i s c u i t s a p p l e s s p r o u t s c h i p s s a u s a g e s e g g s p e a s** and tomatoes all mixed up on the plate.

✎ What do you like in sandwiches? Make a list.

_____

Name _____

✎ Emily and Jack have swept the commas into two piles.
One pile is for commas in lists.
The other pile is for commas with speech marks.
Put commas in the correct places in each sentence.

"This is great " said Jack.

"That wig stinks " laughed Emily.

"Here comes the Queen " whispered Emily.

This powder is for wigs feet and babies' bottoms.

Grey brown cream and white mice ran across the kitchen floor.

"I'd like a mouse as a pet " said Jack.

"Catch the mouse and put it in your pocket " said Emily.

The Queen looked up down left right and then at Jack's pocket.

✎ Make a list of creatures small enough to keep in your pocket.

_____

✎ Make a list of six words that begin with the letter **m**.

_____

Name _____

✎ Jack looks at the menu and says what he wants.
Emily looks at the menu and says what she wants.

Today's Menu

soup   ice cream   fish fingers   cheese   carrot
toast   crackers   apple   milkshake   mash
jacket potato   burger   crisps   chicken wings   curry
chips   doughnuts   cucumber   pizza   rice pudding
apple pie   orange   cereal   chapatti   grapes
rice   sausages   samosa   meat pie   biscuits   seeds

"My four best things will be _____

_____," said Jack.

"My four best things will be _____

_____," said Emily.

✎ Make a list of menu words that begin with the letter **c**.

_____

✎ Make a list of menu words with five letters in them.

_____

✎ On the back of this sheet draw a picture of your
favourite dinner and your favourite pudding.
Write a list of all the different foods.

Name _____

✎ Emily and Jack have been invited to the Queen's banquet.
The food words on the invitation have been squashed together.
Separate the words with commas.

, , , , , , , , , , ,

To start you can choose:

souptoastcucumbermelonprawns or sliced tomatoes.

For the main course you can choose:

chickenwingssausagesmashcabbage or fish fingers.

For pudding you can choose:

bananasgrapesorangesicecreamcookies or cake.

To drink you can choose:

watermilkjuiceteacoffeemilkshake or cola.

To take home you can choose:

chocolatefudgetoffee or even bubblegum.

, , , , , , , , , , ,

✎ Design an invitation card for a banquet on the back of this sheet.
Tell your guests what food there will be and the time and place.

Name _____

✎ Emily and Jack are talking too quickly. They need to slow down and use commas. Write the commas in.

, "I like chips pizza and peas " said Jack. ,

"The fizzy drink has made me burp " said Emily.

, ,

"My gran makes soup pizza and fudge " Jack told Emily.

, ,

"We made biscuits with eggs milk sugar butter and flour " said Emily.

, ,

"Goats chew grass leaves paper and even cloth " said Jack.

, ,

"Vegetarians eat vegetables sprouts nuts cheese eggs and fruit " Emily said.

✎ Make a list of foods you don't like.

_____

✎ Make a list of things a wizard would put in a potion.

_____

Organisational devices

Intended learning

- To know the purpose of a range of organisational devices, including headings, bullet points, highlighting, labelling, alphabetical ordering and symbols.

Preparation and resources

- Put an alphabet strip on display in the classroom.
- Have dictionaries, the register, a copy of the Highway Code and a few maps and newspapers to hand in the classroom.
- Highlighter pens for Activity sheet 1B.
- Blank paper for Activity sheet 2B.
- Copies of a list of class members' names in non-alphabetical order for the cross-curricular activities.

Starting point

Show the class a range of texts which include headings, bullet points, highlighting, labelling, alphabetical ordering and symbols. Maps and the Highway Code are particularly useful for symbols.

Read the story

Before you begin, tell the children that you will be able to read this story properly because it has been properly organised.

Lower order questions

What are the first eight letters of the alphabet?
What are the next eight?
What are the last ten?
What is the fourth letter of the alphabet?
What is the ninth? (And so on.)
What is a symbol?

Higher order questions

Why are dictionaries in alphabetical order?
How are newspaper headings like chapter headings?
Why do people use highlighters?
How would symbols help you in a foreign country?
What are bullet points used for?

Points to note

- Organisational devices are used to make the information easier to understand.
- There should never be so many devices that the text becomes confusing.

Group oral work

Show headings from newspapers. Ask the children what they think each article is about. Are the headings eye-catching and interesting?

With the alphabet strip on display, refer to a dictionary. Ask children to give a rough guess (beginning, middle or end) as to where various words will be found in the dictionary. Start with 'animal', 'zoo', 'monkey' and 'ostrich'. Emphasise that knowing the alphabet saves time.

Discuss why names in registers and phone books are listed alphabetically.

Ask children what signs and symbols they have seen on their way to school. Ask children what signs and symbols they have seen in school.

The activity sheets

Sheets 1A, 1B and 1C

1A This sheet is aimed at children who are emergent readers and need support. The sheet shows six signs. Each one has a symbol but is missing words. The children write the correct words on each sign. Extension – the children write a sentence to say why name tags in clothes are important.

1B This sheet is aimed at more confident readers. The children highlight every animal named in a short story. Extension – the children are asked to write the names of four of the animals they have identified and highlight the vowels. They write two girls' names and two boys' names in alphabetical order, then highlight the girls' names.

1C This sheet is aimed at the able and more able children. In the first set of five sentences there are three relevant to *going to* the zoo. The children identify the three sentences and write them beside the bullet points. In the second set of five sentences, three are relevant to *being at* the zoo. The children identify the three sentences and write them beside the bullet points. Extension – the children bullet point five things they do before going to school.

Sheets 2A, 2B and 2C

2A This sheet is aimed at children who are emergent readers and need support. There are eight blank signs on the sheet arranged in two sets of four. The children write the names of the animals in alphabetical order on each set of signs. Extension – there are an incomplete lower and upper case alphabets for the children to complete.

2B This sheet is aimed at more confident readers. There are six symbols around the page. The children draw road signs in the left section and zoo signs in the right section. Extension – the children are asked to design three signs for their bedroom.

2C This sheet is aimed at the able and more able children. Six headlines and six articles have been muddled up. The children match the headlines to the articles. Extension – the children make up headlines for articles about a school sports day, a bank and a competition.

Plenary

• Each of the activity sheets looks at a different organisational device. Ask children to show and explain their activity sheets.

Cross-curricular activities

Maths

Distribute lists of class members, with the names arranged in non-alphabetical order. Ask children to use a highlighter pen to identify names with more than six letters and then use a different highlighter to identify names with fewer than six letters. Work out how many names are from the first half of the alphabet. Bullet point names with more than three vowels.

Geography

Ask children to design a zoo and show their design in map form.

PSHE

Talk about the advantages of being organised, in the children's daily lives.
Talk about how these rules help keep things organised: stop and wait when people get off a bus; stop talking when the teacher calls for attention; don't push in a crowd.
Talk about the advantages of being organised for fire-fighters, lifeboat crews, train drivers, airport workers and so on.

Time the children fetching an item stored in the correct place and then time them hunting for it when it's been left in the wrong place.

The wild zoo

"Move, or it will crush you!" yelled a man.

Emily and Jack dived out of the way, just in time.

A huge rhino sped past.

"Follow me," called the man, running out of the rhino's cage. Emily and Jack ran after him. As soon as they were out of the cage, the man locked the door behind them.

"What's going on?" asked Jack.

"You're in a zoo," the man replied, "and I'm the zookeeper."

Jack looked in his hands; he was still holding the carved wooden rhinoceros he'd taken from the chest in the loft and Emily was still holding the carved monkey.

"How did we end up in a rhino's cage?" asked Emily. "It nearly killed us!"

"Because," explained the zookeeper, "two monkeys escaped in the night. They've swapped all of the zoo signs around. Everyone's ending up in the wrong places. Everything is so disorganised now. Just look around."

It was true.

Some boys were stranded on the island in the middle of the penguin pool. A girl was riding on a giraffe's back. A family were standing nervously on the roof of the elephant house. And an ice cream van was driving around inside the lions' cage, being chased by two lionesses.

"Why don't you just point the signs back in the right direction?" asked Jack.

"I haven't had a chance," the zookeeper said. "I'm too busy rescuing people. And however fast I run there's no way I can rescue everyone. I need some help."

At that second there was a scream from somewhere in the distance. The zookeeper dashed off to see what had happened.

"It's up to us to help him," said Emily.

Five minutes later, Emily and Jack were at the entrance to the zoo. Emily picked up a map of the zoo. It showed where everything should be.

"OK," said Emily. "Let's get organised. We'll rescue all the people and then we'll point the signs back in the right direction."

"Good idea," replied Jack.

"I'm going to make a list on the back of this map with bullet points so we know exactly what we have to do," said Emily.

Jack nodded, saying, "First we need to help that family off the roof of the elephant house."

"No, they're safe for a bit," said Emily. "I think first we should get the ice cream van out of the lions' cage."

"You're right," agreed Jack. "Ice cream van first, family on the roof second."

"Third is the girl on the giraffe's back," said Emily.

"And fourth," added Jack, "we should help the boys out of the penguin pool."

The wild zoo

Emily grabbed a pencil and quickly made four bullet points:

> • Ice cream van in lions' cage
>
> • Family on elephant house roof
>
> • Girl on giraffe
>
> • Boys in penguin pool

...then she and Jack ran as fast as they could.

First they distracted the lions so the driver could get his ice cream van out of their cage.

Second they leant a ladder up against the elephant house.

"Thanks!" shouted the family as they clambered down.

Next they dragged a trampoline beside the giraffe so that the girl could safely jump off its neck.

Finally, they lobbed rubber rings to the boys on the island in the penguin pool. The boys used the rings to swim across the pool and climbed out. They were soaking wet but happy to be back on solid ground.

"Now for the signs," Jack said.

Using the map, Emily and Jack hurried around the zoo, pushing and knocking signs so they pointed in the right direction again.

The sign that said THIS WAY TO THE MONKEY HOUSE was under a table in the café.

As Emily and Jack pulled it out...

Wham! Clonk! – two coconuts hit them on their backs!

They looked round. Up in the trees behind them they saw two monkeys about to throw more coconuts at them.

"That's them!" shouted Jack. "I bet they're the ones who changed all the signs round and caused this chaos. Let's go after them!"

But just as the monkeys took aim with more coconut shells Emily and Jack were surrounded by a blue mist and felt themselves being pulled down at an incredible speed.

They landed with a bump on the attic floor.

"Hey, you two! There's too much jumping going on up there!" Mum shouted up to them. "Come down now. Coats on – we need to get going."

"Where are we going, Mum?" asked Emily, as she and Jack walked into the kitchen.

"You can't have forgotten," Mrs Ashcroft said. "We're going to the zoo."

Name _____

✎ The labels have fallen off the signs.

Write the words on the signs to match the symbols.

CAR PARK	TEA SHOP	ICECREAM

LOST CHILDREN	ELEPHANT RIDES	TELEPHONE

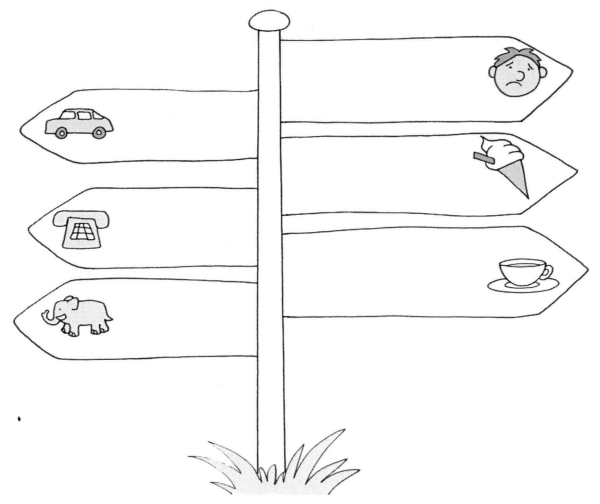

✎ Why is it important to have name tags in your clothes?

_____

✎ On the back of the sheet draw a picture of yourself.
Label all your clothes.

Name _____

✏️ Highlight every animal named in this story.

A kangaroo had hopped on the giraffe's back.

Monkeys were leaping everywhere.

There were pigs in the penguin pool.

There were rabbits in the elephant house.

The icecream van was in the lions' cage!

The brown bear lumbered past.

A huge rhino sped by.

"Help!" cried the keeper.

✏️ **a e i o u**

Write the names of four animals from the story.
Highlight the vowels in the words.

_____   _____   _____   _____

✏️ Write two boys' names and two girls' names
in alphabetical order. Highlight the girls' names.

_____

_____

_____

_____

Activity sheet 1C

Name _____

✎ Jack is making a plan to **go to the zoo**. He has five sentences.
Choose three important sentences and bullet point them in order.

| Look at the animals. | Get a ticket. | Watch a video. |

| Go through the gate. | He is my friend. |

● _____

● _____

● _____

✎ Emily is planning their time **at the zoo**. She has five
sentences. Choose three important sentences and bullet
point them in order.

| Feed the parrots. | Tidy my room. | Clean my teeth. |

| Buy a bag of seed. | Watch the monkeys. |

● _____

● _____

● _____

✎ On the back of this sheet make a list of five bullet points,
saying what you do before you come to school.

Name _____

✎ Emily and Jack each have a list of animals.

Write the animals on the signs in alphabetical order.

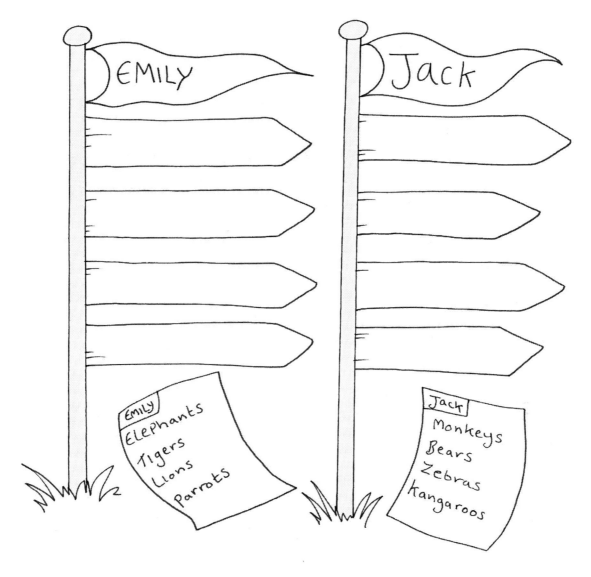

✎ Complete the alphabets.

One is in capital letters. One is in lower case.

a b __ d e __ g h i __ k l m

n o __ q r __ t __ v w x __ __

A B __ D E F __ H __ J K __ __

N O __ Q __ S T __ V W __ __ Z

✎ Jack and Emily find signs scattered around the zoo.
Some are road signs and some are zoo signs.
Help them sort out the signs.

ROAD SIGNS	ZOO SIGNS

✎ On separate pieces of paper, design three signs for your bedroom.

Name _____

✎ The monkeys have torn the headlines off the newspaper stories.
Help Jack and Emily match them up.

(1.) **BIG CATS ESCAPE**   (2.) **ZOO CLOSED**

(3.) **ROADS MELT**   (4.) **MONKEY BUSINESS**

(5.) **DINOSAURS DISCOVERED**   (6.) **SAVED**

An elephant rescued a baby when it fell into the penguins' pool.

Headline number ◯

There was a riot at the zoo when visitors found the gates locked.

Headline number ◯

The wheels of cars, lorries and buses stuck to the streets.

Headline number ◯

Several tyrannosaurs have been found in the jungle.

Headline number ◯

Drunken monkeys were seen eating stolen wine gums.

Headline number ◯

Police and fire services were called to capture the cats.

Headline number ◯

✎ Write a headline about a school sports day.

_____

Write a headline about a bank.

_____

Write a headline about a competition.

_____

Speech and thought bubbles

Intended learning
- To know that speech and thoughts can be written in speech and thought bubbles.

Preparation and resources
- Make available books and comics with speech and thought bubbles.
- On the board draw (or stick) a picture of a person. Draw a large speech bubble and thought bubble coming from the person's head.
- Prepare a strip of paper for each child by cutting A4 into four strips along the long side.
- Write names of a variety of geographical features on the board (separately from the person with the speech and thought bubbles). For example: *river   mountain   forest   valley   sandy beach*
- Magazines, scissors and glue for Activity sheet 2C.

Starting point
Show the children the bubbles on the board. Explain that when speech is written in this way there is no need for words like *said*, *shouted*, *mumbled* and so on.

Read the story
Explain to the children what a canyon is before reading the story. When reading the story give extra emphasis to the spoken words in the speech bubbles.

Lower order questions
Where were Emily and Jack?
How did they get out of the canyon?
What is a speech bubble?
How do you make a bubble with bubblegum?

Higher order questions
Why are speech bubbles useful in comics?
Explain the difference between speaking and thinking.
Why is it that some people, like teachers and parents, can often guess what you're thinking about?

Points to note
- Demonstrate that it works better if you write the words first, then draw the bubbles round them.
- Point out that speech bubbles have a tail and thought bubbles a series of little clouds trailing towards the speaker.

Group oral work
Ask the class to be silent. Now tell them to imagine they are going on a trip. Ask them, *in silence*, to imagine where they are going, choosing from the suggestions on the board, and then write it down on a piece of paper. Now invite different children in turn, still without talking, to stand and show everyone their piece of paper. The rest of the class say, for example, "She is thinking about a trip to a river."

Look at the picture of the person on the board. Write different statements in the speech bubble; for example, "What a lovely dress," or "I'm not scared of spiders." Ask the class to imagine what the person might be *thinking* as opposed to what they are *saying*. Point out that people often don't say exactly what they think.

The activity sheets

Sheets 1A, 1B and 1C
1A This sheet is aimed at children who are emergent readers and need support. There are six sentences and six thought bubbles. Three belong to Emily and three to Jack. The children identify who is thinking what and write the thoughts in the bubbles. Extension – write a thought about a fire engine and a thought about home time.

1B This sheet is aimed at more confident readers. Written on trees are various words, some of which are exclamations. The children are asked to choose six exclamations and write them in the thought bubbles, remembering the exclamation marks. Extension – write the teacher's thoughts in a thought bubble.

1C This sheet is aimed at the able and more able children. There are nine thoughts; three each for Emily, Jack and Mum. The children decide who is thinking what and write the thoughts in the correct bubbles. Extension – the children draw self-portraits with a speech bubble containing their playtime thoughts.

Sheets 2A, 2B and 2C
2A This sheet is aimed at children who are emergent readers and need support. There are six sentences and three thought bubbles. One bubble belongs to Mum, one to Jack and one to Emily. The children decide who is thinking what and write two thoughts in each bubble. Extension – the children are asked to think about their favourite food and

draw a picture of themselves, including their food thought in a thought bubble.

2B This sheet is aimed at more confident readers. The children write thoughts in bubbles about finding treasure. Extension – the children make a list of special things to keep in a treasure chest, remembering commas between the items.

2C This sheet is aimed at able and more able children. On the sheet is a brief description of what Jack, Emily and Mum are thinking about. For each character children write two sentences in their speech or thought bubble. Extension – cut pictures of faces from magazines. Draw speech bubbles from their faces and write words in the bubbles.

Plenary

- The children show their finished activity sheets. Choose children to read out their speech and thought bubbles.
- Ask children to explain how the reader knows which bubble belongs to which character.
- Ask children to explain the difference between a speech bubble and a thought bubble.

Cross-curricular activities

Art

Make a display of children's photographs, each with a completed thought bubble.

Maths

Look at the different shapes used to create speech bubbles and thought bubbles.

Science

Investigate bubbles. Set out a jar of cold tap water, a jar of warm water, a jar of warm water with a few drops of oil added and a jar of salty water. Add half a teaspoon of washing-up liquid to each jar. Whisk thoroughly and discuss the results.

Give each child two pieces of white cloth or white paper hand towels. First, ask the children to wet their hands under the cold tap and dry them on the first towel. Next, ask the children to wash their hands with soap, making a lather (bubbles), then dry. Compare the towels. Discuss how washing with soap and making bubbles is more effective than using water alone.

Bubble up

"Those look really weird," whispered Emily, as she picked up two very old packets of bubblegum from the chest in the loft. She kept one for herself and handed the other to Jack.

A split second later, they were surrounded by a blue mist and felt themselves being pulled upwards at an incredible speed.

They found themselves facing each other on opposite sides of a very deep canyon. They were standing on narrow ledges. If they stepped too far forward, they would fall into the canyon.

It was a boiling hot day. Far below on the canyon floor a light wind sent the dust swirling in thin clouds.

Jack opened his mouth to call across to Emily. He thought he was shouting but no sound came out.

He saw Emily trying to shout across at him but the same thing was happening to her. She looked like she was calling but there was no sound. Her voice had fallen silent.

Carefully, Jack sat down on the narrow ledge and looked over the side. It really was a very, very deep canyon.

He pulled out the packet of old bubblegum from the loft and popped a piece into his mouth. It tasted a bit like lemon crossed with strawberries.

"This bubblegum tastes good," he thought. After chewing for a while he decided to give shouting another go. He'd tell Emily about the tasty bubblegum.

He opened his mouth to shout what he'd been thinking when a very strange thing happened. His voice still didn't make any sound but instead a bubble floated out of his mouth.

It was quite small, only pea-sized to begin with, but as it floated across the canyon it slowly grew bigger and bigger. Jack looked at the bubble in amazement.

Inside it were the words he had tried to shout:

This bubblegum tastes good.

Jack couldn't believe it! He watched the bubble float higher and higher until it disappeared into the sky.

Would Emily's gum do the same thing? He shouted at her to try the gum but no noise came from his mouth. Instead, like before, a small bubble appeared. As the bubble grew bigger the words he had been thinking appeared inside it:

Try the gum.

And then this bubble too floated up and out of sight.

Emily quickly opened her pack of gum and put a piece in her mouth.

A few seconds later, Jack watched as Emily opened her mouth to shout at him.

From her mouth came a bubble carrying the words:

It tastes really good Jack!

Jack thought about this for a while and then suddenly it hit him. He opened his mouth again. A bubble came out saying:

We are making speech bubbles.

Bubble up

Emily suddenly burst out laughing and a new bubble appeared from her mouth.

You're right! When you write the words that someone says, you can write them in a speech bubble!

Yes! said Jack's next bubble. **Like in cartoon strips and comic books.**

Emily nodded across the canyon and then another bubble came from her mouth.

OK, we know about speech bubbles but how are we going to get out of here?

Jack stood up and looked around. As he looked down into the darkness of the canyon he had an idea. He opened his mouth and a bubble came out saying:

Emily, watch me and copy what I do!

As this bubble grew, Jack wrapped his arms round it. He started floating out across the canyon.

Emily's eyes were wide with amazement. Out of her mouth came a bubble saying:

I'm copying you!

As this bubble grew, she grabbed hold, clung on tightly and felt herself rising in the air.

As Emily and Jack's bubbles floated slowly up the canyon they moved nearer to each other every second.

Up and up they floated and were nearly at the top of the canyon when **bump**!

They crashed into each other and immediately the bubbles burst. Suddenly Emily and Jack were surrounded by a blue mist and were being pulled downwards at an incredible speed.

They found themselves in a heap on the floor next to the chest in the loft.

"Come down from the loft now, you two!" Emily's mum shouted up at them.

"Just coming," shouted back Emily, chewing her gum and delighted that she'd found her voice again.

"Get rid of that horrid gum," her mum replied. "I know you're chewing it – I can't understand a word you're saying."

Name _____

 Emily and Jack are in a canyon.
Write Emily's thoughts in her thought bubbles.
Write Jack's thoughts in his thought bubbles.

"Will we get out?" Emily wondered.
Emily thought, "I'm scared."
She thought, "Jack will know what to do."

Jack had an idea – "Chew gum!"
"Watch me," thought Jack.
Jack thought, "I'm going up!"

 Write in one bubble what you think when you hear a fire engine and in the other what you think at home time.

Name _____

✎ Emily and Jack are very excited as they float out of the canyon.
Find six exclamation words and write them in the thought bubbles.
Remember to put an exclamation mark after the words.

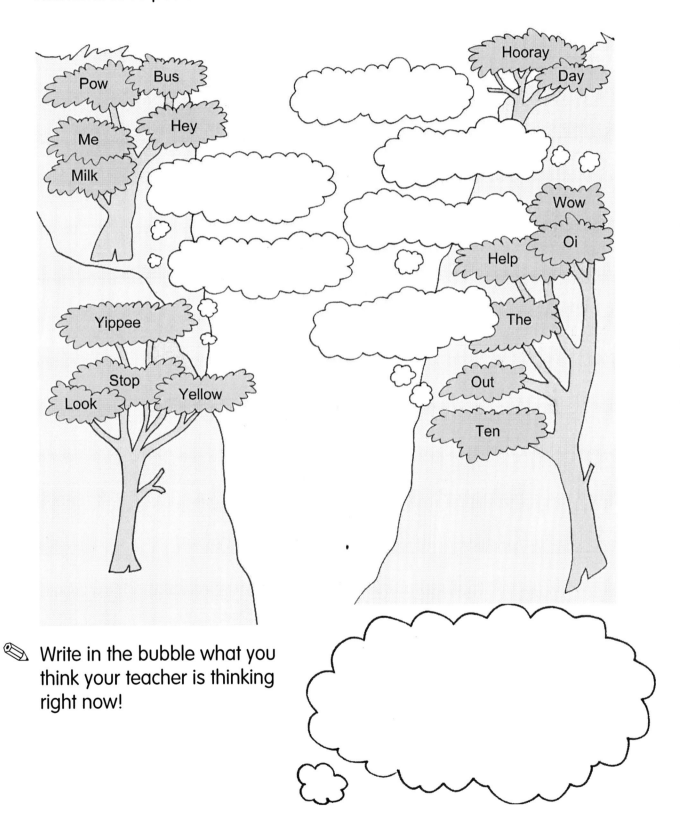

✎ Write in the bubble what you think your teacher is thinking right now!

Name _____

 Who is thinking what?

Write each thought in the correct person's thought bubbles.

They'll get dirty in the loft.

She's not like other girls.

His grandad was a sailor.

Soon I'll be as tall as him.

Emily runs as fast as me.

Jack makes me laugh.

I'll give them pizza for tea.

Emily's mum never shouts.

I expect they're getting hungry.

Emily   **Jack**   **Mum**

 On the back of this sheet draw a picture of yourself.

In a thought bubble write what you were thinking at the last playtime.

Name _____

✎ Emily, Jack and Mum are thinking.
Write their thoughts in the bubbles.

"Where are they?" thought Mum.

"Is it dark?" wondered Jack.

"We mustn't touch the box," thought Emily.

Jack thought, "This is spooky."

"I'll call them down," Mum decided.

Emily thought, "I can hear Mum calling."

Jack

Emily

Mum

✎ Think about your favourite food. On the back of this sheet draw a picture
of yourself thinking about the food. Draw the food in a thought bubble.

Name _____

✎ Emily and Jack's adventures happen because of the things they find in an old wooden chest.
What would you think if you found a box marked **TREASURE**?

Write your thoughts in these thought bubbles.

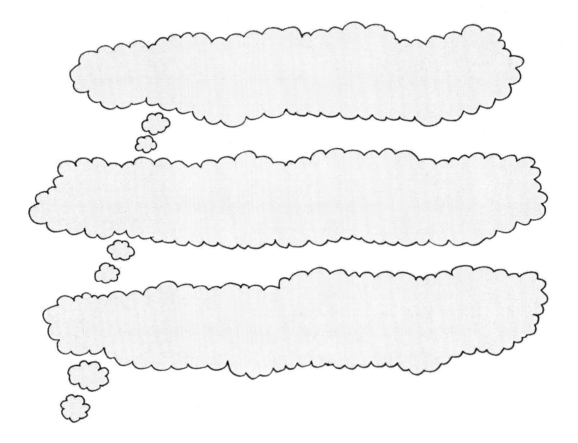

✎ Make a list of five special things you would keep in a treasure chest. Don't forget to use commas in the list.

_____

_____

Name _____

✎ That night Emily's mum found bubblegum trodden into the carpet.
Write what she said to Emily and Jack in the speech bubble.

✎ That night Emily thought
about the chest in the loft.
Write two of her thoughts in
the bubble.

✎ That night Jack thought
about their adventures.
Write two of his thoughts
in the bubble.

✎ Cut out faces from magazines and stick them into your book.
Write what each person is saying in a speech bubble.

PUNCTUATION CHALLENGE

The weapons in **Polta and the space war** remind you that...

EXCLAMATION MARKS MAKE WORDS
STRONG AND POWERFUL.

Hooks to catch words in **Diving in the deep** remind you to...

USE SPEECH MARKS TO CATCH SPOKEN WORDS.

Finding the question words in **Escape from the tower** reminds you that...

THERE ARE MANY DIFFERENT WAYS TO ASK QUESTIONS.

Using curls for commas in **The Queen's banquet** reminds you to...

USE COMMAS IN LISTS AND WITH SPEECH MARKS.

The wild zoo was a mess but...

ORGANISATIONAL DEVICES GET THINGS ORGANISED.

The bubbles in **Bubble up** remind you that...

SPEECH AND THOUGHT CAN BE WRITTEN IN BUBBLES.